TC's Chr
Discovery

To Harriet and Sylvie

Best Wishes

Gillian A. Cornfield.

Gillian A Cornfield

Acknowledgements

My love and thanks go to Dilys, Julian and Louise for all their encouragement and steadfast support.

Thank you to all the Bournemouth schoolchildren who acted as my 'young editors' on the first draft of this book.

My thanks to Tina Webb, Publishing Manager, NCH, for all her input and enthusiasm.

NCH, the children's charity, helps children and young people facing difficulties or challenges in their lives. All our services are unique as they are developed in response to specific local needs, but they are all run in partnership with communities and local agencies. We all share a common vision: to make sure that every child has a chance to live their life to the full.

For further information, please contact our **Supporter Helpline on 08457 626579** (calls charged at local rate, open 9am–5pm Monday to Friday).

Website: www.nch.org.uk

Registered charity no. 1097940 / company no. 4764232

the children's charity

Hi, Children-peoples, I'm so glad you've opened the book, it's great to meet you. My name is TC. Now, I expect you're thinking that this stands for, "Totally Cool." Well, as you can see, I am a totally cool cat, but the truth is, TC stands for "Totally Confused."

When I was a kitten-baby, my silly peoples called me Annabella, because they thought I was a girl kitten.

Then they found out I was a boy and called me TC, because they thought I must be totally confused.

Now, I was never mixed up. I knew I was a boy kitten, but peoples get funny ideas and the name TC stuck.

Now let's get one thing straight, I want you to know that I am real, not just some made up character for a book. I'd love to be a famous cat, but my peoples say I'm just an ordinary little mog, but there is only one of me, and that makes me special.

I live in the Tilly room of my house. I think peoples call it a Utility room.

It is a place where my peoples wash their clothes in a thing called a washing machine. Can't understand why they do that, as I love my Tilly room dirty, covered in my fur, my smells, and lots of dirty paw prints.

Come and have a look around.

This is my bed – a beautiful old duvet, and I have three ships. I'm not altogether sure what they are for, but they look wicked, don't they?

I have one really good mate, Chris Mouse. He is a grey, ordinary little house mouse.

He broke into my Tilly room a few years ago, through the hole behind the washing machine, where the waste pipe is.

When I first saw him, I was pretty miffed, but I was too tired to catch him, and he didn't bother me much. Now we are good mates, and he knows that I'm the boss in the Tilly room.

I belong to Louise-peoples.

When I was a kitten-baby, she was a little girl-peoples, but now she is grown up and is called a student.

As you children-peoples know, life changes, and it has changed for us cats too.

Being a pet is my job.

You have to be there for your peoples, let them stroke you, make them laugh (I chase my tail, that never fails to get a laugh), calm them down when they get stressed – and boy, do they get stressed sometimes! I get lovely wet food, so being a pet is a pretty nifty job.

My life was just ace,

until one day in November when I overheard my peoples talking.

"Louise," said Mum-peoples, "Time's going on, and I think we must start planning for Christmas Day. There is a lot of work to do, and we must start the preparations early. Make a list of all our friends, who we want to send Christmas cards to. I've bought the cards, and you can start writing them, wishing everyone a happy Christmas Day."

8

"Chris Mouse Day? Chris Mouse Day? Why are my peoples having a special day for Chris Mouse? I must have made a mistake."

My head was reeling. It must be one of those birthday-type days. You know, peoples have a special day to celebrate when they were born, but why Chris Mouse day, why not TC day?

I rushed out to my Tilly room and yelled out to Chris, "Chris, when's your birthday?"

"I haven't got one TC."

"You must have because you've been born, you silly mouse. My peoples are having a special day for you."

"Are they TC? I must be important."

"No you're not. I must have got it wrong. I'm going back into the house to get more information."

I made my way into the family room, only to find Louise-peoples sitting on the floor surrounded by all sorts of cards and I went to have a closer look.

"Hello, TC, I've got to write all these Chris Mouse cards, so you'll have to be a good cat."

Be a good cat? Was she joking?

I had a good paw at the cards, and saw that they had a lot of pretty pictures on them, but every one said "Happy Chris Mouse Day!"

You children people get bad hair days; well I was having a bad cat day. I got into trouble messing around with all the cards, so Louise-peoples sent me out.

The next day, I found Mum-peoples wrapping up lots of presents.

There was red, blue and green paper, coloured string and beautiful bows.

"I wonder if there is one for me."

Then I tried to get into one of the presents.

I jumped right on to the table to get a better look.

"Get down TC," said Mum-peoples. "If you're going to stay in, you'll have to behave. I've got lots of Chris Mouse presents to wrap up, and I don't need you misbehaving."

Chris Mouse presents! Not again, I ran into the garden to look for Chris, and found him behind the dustbin.

"Chris."

"Hi, TC."

"Shush, and listen to me. Mum-peoples is wrapping up Chris Mouse presents."

"Really, TC, but I don't think I need anything."

"Not for you, you daft mouse, presents for all the peoples in the family to celebrate Chris Mouse day, your birthday."

"But they don't know me, TC."

"Well they must know you, or they wouldn't be having Chris Mouse day. I think it's a disgrace my peoples celebrating your birthday."

"Don't be mad with me, TC, let's go back to the Tilly room."

"You mean MY Tilly room. No, Chris, I want to be on my own. I'm going to get some peace on my duvet and try to get my head around things."

I went for a long sleep, woke up feeling a huge rumble in my tummy.

I looked through my Tilly room window into the kitchen to see Mum-peoples cooking, and I smelled lovely smells.

I pushed open the kitchen door with my paw and jumped up on to a chair to see what was on the table. Mmm, chocolate, cream.

"TC," said Mum-peoples, "I'll feed you in a minute, but you'll have to wait till I've finished cooking. Would you like a lick of cream?"

Yum, my tongue didn't need a second invitation. It wrapped itself around Mum-people's finger.

"That's enough now, TC, I've got to see to the Chris Mouse pudding."

WHAT? I nearly fell off the chair. CHRIS MOUSE PUDDING! Oh my goodness, they've cooked him! They've put Chris in a pudding!

Suddenly, I didn't feel hungry any more, and I ran out to my Tilly room, and jumped up on to my duvet. I know Chris got on my nerves from time to time, but I didn't want him to end up in a pudding!

THUD! A little grey body landed on my duvet from the top of the freezer.

"CHRIS! I thought you'd been cooked in a pudding!"

"What's a pudding, TC?"

"It's a sort of cake, hot cake."

Little Chris's whiskers were quivering with excitement. "Your peoples have named a pudding after me. That's groovy."

"Be quiet. I don't want to hear any more about Chris Mouse pudding, or anything else to do with you. Do you understand?"

"Please, TC, don't be cross."

Next day, Saturday morning, life was looking up, and I was sitting on the windowsill behind the sofa, looking out of the window. The sun was streaming on to my nose, and I was feeling very relaxed.

I heard the car pull into the drive, and I ran to meet Dad-peoples. That's another pet duty, running to meet your peoples when they come home. I looked at the car, and there was something green and bushy in the back of it. Dad-peoples opened the car door, and he pulled out a tree!

Yes, a tree! A real tree!

What on earth was he doing with a tree?

Dad-peoples walked towards the house carrying the tree.

He can't be taking it inside, but yes, he was walking towards the front door. Now, he often brings Mum-peoples flowers, but he's never brought her a tree! She hasn't got a vase big enough to put it in. Oh dear, Dad-peoples has finally lost the plot! Trees live in the garden. Well, this I've got to see. Boy, is Mum-peoples going to be cross!

I beat Dad-peoples through the front door and waited.

"Is anybody home?" he shouted. "Come and see what I've got."

Louise-peoples ran downstairs, and Mum-peoples appeared from the kitchen.

"Oh, what a beautiful Chris Mouse tree. That will look spectacular in the hall."

I just don't believe this, it's all to do with that mouse again. This is really winding me up.

After lunch, Dad-peoples brought two large brown boxes into the hall.

Umm, interesting. I'd like to have a nose in them.

22

Louise-peoples pulled out gold string, which she called "tinsel," and there were lots of gold and silver balls, little drums, hearts and bells.

This was great fun. I had a rummage in the box, pawed the balls, and pulled the tinsel with my teeth.

Then Mum-peoples said, "Don't let TC touch the Chris Mouse angel and the Chris Mouse lights."

Too late, I'd found the angel and picked her up in my mouth.

Then I ran behind the tree, and pinged the lights with my teeth.

I think it's called "destructive behaviour." You do destructive behaviour when you want to make your peoples cross.

Gosh, did it work!

Dad-people's hands grabbed me, and I found myself flying through the air. He put me out into the Tilly room.

I found Chris curled up by the radiator.

"Hey, Chris, how do you know the Chris Mouse angel?"

"I don't know what an angel is, TC."

"As if! I've had enough of you telling porkies. You must know her, you dozy mouse, if she's named after you."

"Well I don't, TC."

"Oh, go away. I wish they had put you in that pudding. If I hear one more peoples mention Chris Mouse day, I'll give them a good scratch."

That evening, all my peoples were watching television in the Family room, and Dad-peoples brought me in and put me on his lap. He stroked me. I sat there wagging my tail furiously.

"No purr tonight, TC?" said Louise-peoples. "You look really grumpy."

Grumpy? That word didn't even come close to how I was feeling. I expect you children-peoples have heard your grown-up-peoples say they've reached the end of their tether. Well I'd reached the end of my tail, I was so cross.

"Come on, TC, it's Chris Mouse Eve, tomorrow. Dad, let's show TC the Chris Mouse tree and the stable scene."

Dad-peoples carried me into the hall.

On the hall table, I saw some tiny figures, in a shed thing; that must be the stable.

"Look, TC, there are Mary, Joseph and baby Jesus, lying in the manger. Jesus is the Christ child. That's why we have Christmas Day, to celebrate his birthday. Christmas is a time for giving."

My ears pricked up.

Christ child! Christmas! Oh, it's CHRISTMAS DAY not Chris Mouse day. A big smile crept over my pussycat face. They couldn't see it, but you can, can't you?

I wanted to take a closer look, and this time, I behaved.

Look, can you see Mary, Joseph and the baby Jesus? If you look carefully, you can see a shepherd and three very grand kings.

Now everything made sense. All the celebrations were for Jesus' birthday; what a special baby. Wait till I tell Chris, that will wipe the smile off his little mouse face.

The next day was Christmas Eve, and all my peoples were busy preparing for Christmas Day. Late that night, Louise-peoples gave me a top-up snack, duck and goose – my favourite!

"TC, we're all going to church tonight, to sing carols to welcome in Christmas Day. I've got to go now, so be a good cat."

"Louise," called Mum-peoples, "Come on, or we'll be late. Will you leave all the lights on, please?"

I heard the car drive off, and I went to look for Chris. Chris was on his pipe.

"Chris!"

"Go away TC, I've been hiding from you, because I'm fed up with you giving me a hard time over my birthday, which I know nothing about."

"Oh, that's all finished with now, little mate. I've come to explain. It's Jesus' birthday, not yours."

"You mean you made a mistake, TC?"

"Um, no. Well, yes. No, never mind that. I've got something wonderful to show you. Come on, we're going inside the house, all my peoples are out, and I want to show you baby Jesus."

We made our way into the hall, and I jumped up on to the table.

"Come on, Chris, keep up!"

"I can't get up there, TC.

"Of course you can. Run up the leg."

33

We sat in front of the crib.

"Look at the beautiful baby, Chris. He is the Christ child, and tomorrow is his birthday, Christmas Day."

"Gosh he's something else."

"Yes he is, and I'm sorry I've given you a load of grief, Chris, I got the wrong end of the stick about Christmas."

"Forget it, TC. We're friends and we won't argue any more."

Chris scampered up on to the stable roof.

"Get down, Chris, you might break something."

"I'm looking to see if there's a mouse in the stable."

"Of course, there isn't a mouse. Jesus would've had a cat."

"TC, there isn't a cat, I can only see a lamb"

"There would've been a cat. Cats are very important."

"TC, I thought we weren't going to argue any more!"

"We're not. Well, not tonight. Happy Christmas, Chris."

"Happy Christmas, TC."

PS. I hope all you children-peoples get some lovely presents. I got a present. Look on the front cover, and you will see me trying to open it.

Now turn this page to find out what it is.

See? A beautiful blanket.

Happy Christmas, everyone. Hope to see you all again soon.

Love, TC